Soccer Is Our Game

By Leila Boyle Gemme

Photographs by Roberta Caliger

 CHILDRENS PRESS, CHICAGO

Library of Congress Cataloging in Publication Data

Gemme, Leila B.
  Soccer is our game.

  SUMMARY: An introduction to soccer in simple text
and photographs.
    1. Soccer—Juvenile literature.   [1. Soccer]
I. Caliger, Roberta. II. Title.
GV943.25.G42   796.33'42   79-13245
ISBN 0-516-03615-7

1 2 3 4 5 6 7 8 9 10 11 12 R 85 84 83 82 81 80 79

Soccer is our game.

We like to run and kick.

We learn to kick.

Our hands may not touch the ball.

Our coach shows us how to kick.

We have to dribble the ball.
It is fun to make short kicks.

We pass the ball with long kicks.

We try to hit high balls with our heads.
It is not easy.

We wear shin guards to protect our legs.

Our games begin with a coin flip.

To score, we try to
kick the ball into the cage.

The other team tries to steal the ball.

At half time we enjoy our oranges.

The coach gives us some help.

During the game, he cheers for the team.

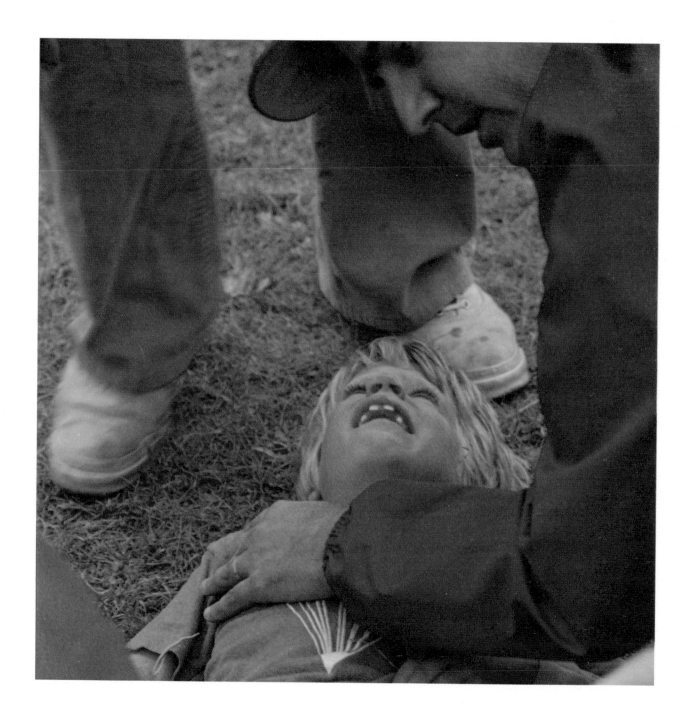

Sometimes soccer hurts!

But most of the time
it is a lot of fun.

The game is over.
We cheer the other team.

Soccer players
are proud.
Our game is hard
and fast and fun.

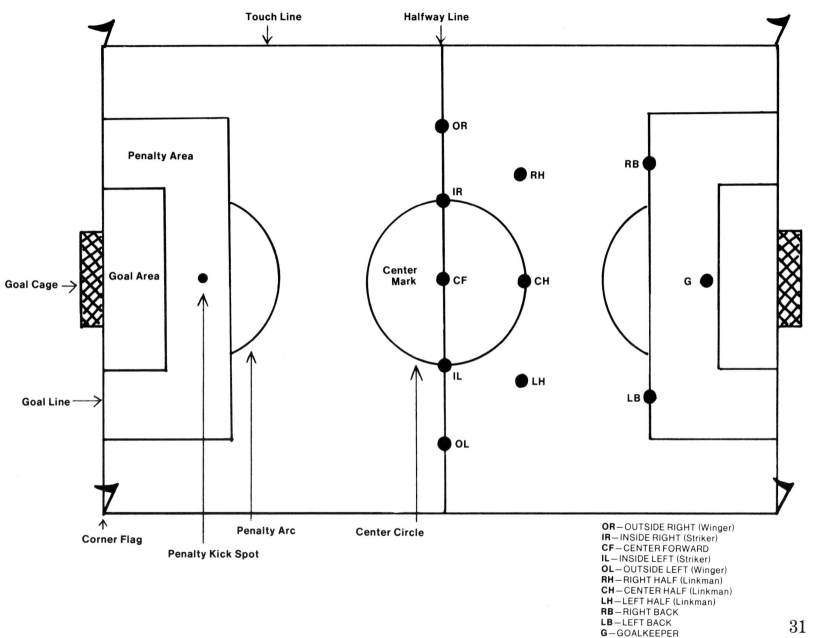

Touch Line

Halfway Line

Penalty Area

Goal Cage →

Goal Area

Center Mark

OR

IR

RH

CF

CH

IL

LH

OL

RB

G

LB

Goal Line →

Corner Flag

Penalty Arc

Center Circle

Penalty Kick Spot

OR—OUTSIDE RIGHT (Winger)
IR—INSIDE RIGHT (Striker)
CF—CENTER FORWARD
IL—INSIDE LEFT (Striker)
OL—OUTSIDE LEFT (Winger)
RH—RIGHT HALF (Linkman)
CH—CENTER HALF (Linkman)
LH—LEFT HALF (Linkman)
RB—RIGHT BACK
LB—LEFT BACK
G—GOALKEEPER

31

About the Author

Leila Boyle Gemme was a high school teacher for several years before turning to writing. She has lived in Connecticut, California, and Illinois. The subjects of her works are varied. Among other things, she has written about the sports world, entertainers, and the space program.

About the Photographer:

Roberta Caliger, the mother of four children, operates a freelance studio in Crystal Lake, Illinois, called Birdie's Eye. Her other interests include dance and crafts.